DIARY OF THE
ANGRY I

By
Sabrina Ne'Chelle

Copyright

Diary of the Angry I © 2020

Sabrina Ne'Chelle

Printed in the United States of America

ISBN: 978-0-578-69529-7

Names have been changed to protect individuals' privacy.

This book does not replace the advice of a medical professional.

These are my memories, from my perspective, and I have tried to represent events as faithfully as possible.

Scriptures marked KJV are taken from the KING JAMES VERSION (KJV): KING JAMES VERSION, public domain.

FOREWORD

Forgiveness is described as the intentional and voluntary process by which a victim undergoes changes in feelings and attitude regarding an offense and lets go of negative emotions, such as vengefulness, with an increased ability to wish the offender well. Merriam-Webster Dictionary describes forgiveness as "the action or process of forgiving or being forgiven." What I find most interesting is the fact that forgiveness is a plural noun, a word used to describe more than one person's involvement.

Forgiveness isn't for the other person; it is indeed for you. It gives the victim the power to let go, move on, heal and be set free. The two words "I forgive" is even more powerful. It now positions a noun--person, place or thing--in front of a plural noun, which is used to describe more than one person, signifying that I have forgiven the people, places and things of my past that caused me pain. I have healed. I have moved on. It also speaks to the essence of who I am, my purpose. It was necessary for me to go through trials. God knew every mistake I would make, raised me up with a standard, gave me victory and for this I give him praise. My past does not dictate my future.

I hope you learn to forgive too. Your destiny depends on it!

SPECIAL THANKS AND DEDICATION

I thank God for being Lord over my life, for leading me to paths of righteousness, and for leading me into my promise land.

I want to thank my sister, Dorothy Cherell, who always told me I could do anything.

I would like to especially thank my best friend, Theresa Fisher, for being a true friend.

I would also like to dedicate this book to my childhood friend, Shonda Corbett. I would've never made it without you. Thank you for everything!

TABLE OF CONTENTS

CHAPTER 1
THE ANGRY I

Many things have happened in my life that caused me to live in a constant state of anger. I was angry about anything, everything, and at everyone. I was angry with God for the life I lived, the parents I had, the marriages that went sour, and for the relationships that went as quickly as they came. I faced one major disappointment after another. I was angry for having a schizophrenic mother who wasn't ever capable of having a normal conversation or giving me advice at the most critical seasons in my life. I was angry with my deceased father for beating my schizophrenic mother like he was training for a fight with Mahammad Ali and using her head as his daily punching bag. I'd watched my mother be a faithful wife, mother, active church member, and college student. On graduation day, she received the highest honors one could receive. So, I often wondered how the same woman, whom I'd watched wear the title of *College President* and a silver and gold tassel around her neck for being an *A* student, could allow a man to deteriorate her mind to a level where brilliance no longer existed. I was angry that, although I said I would never walk in my mother's shoes or be like my mother, I too married a man who was just as cruel and heartless as my father.

I was furious with my father, who would buy so little food, that at the age of nine, during an annual physical, a physician pulled my skin from my bones and informed my mother about how bad our lives really were. I was suffering from malnutrition. She was in denial, and I was angry that there was only enough food to feed us for three days out of a seven-day week. I was also angry that the food that we did eat within those three days could be compared to slop from a farm.

I was furious with my mom for moving us away from our family and friends into a predominantly white neighborhood and a house she could not afford, where the abuse began. I was angry with her for removing me from a school where I was surrounded by children whose skin and features resembled mine. I was angry with my teacher for being angry with the students whose ethnicities were not her own. I was angry at that school for not having a cafeteria, and I was angry that we were instead fed moldy sandwiches for lunch, which now meant I was being starved both at home and in school. And yes, I was angry that no one took notice of how frail I became.

I was angry that the same family members, who physically, sexually, mentally and spiritually abused me, screamed at me about salvation and God during every church service.

I am Sabrina Ne'Chelle, and this is the story of my life, The Angry I.

"Sabrina, are you up?" my cousin screamed. She would knock on my door at seven o'clock each summer morning to start our routine of playing at the community park.

My mother would tell my cousin and childhood friend, "Could you have come a little later?"

She, in return, would tell my mother, "Yes, that's what my mother said, so I waited an hour."

"Okay," my mother would laugh, "Go ahead, Sabrina," then I would be gone for the day. I was known for being Joyce's youngest daughter of two, with long, auburn-colored hair that hung down my back, cinnamon skin, pink lips, and young tender hips. I would run all day. Every day for six years, my cousin, childhood friends and I would play on the swings to see who could swing the highest, run up the rocket sliding board, play a girls-against-boys game of tag, and catch a girl kissing another girl in the cemetery adjacent to the neighborhood park. I made sure I never got caught.

But something soon changed. My mother found out I had a heart condition that required surgery. Months later, my maternal grandmother, who always seemed to end family quarrels, made us admit when we were wrong, and made us apologize and be loving to one another, died. My maternal grandfather died shortly after the passing of my grandmother, so my mother decided it was best for us to move to the nearest town where we knew no one since my grandmother's death caused my mother to be estranged from the family.

I was in the fourth grade. I was petrified. I grew up in the small but overly populated, culturally diverse city of Camden, New Jersey. I lived there during the 1970s, an era when it was acceptable for any adult to correct your children if that adult witnessed your children misbehaving. They would sit on the stoop, tell your momma they saw you doing something wrong, then smile and tell you how cute you looked with your greasy, 'baby hair edges' just to ease the pain of the whooping you got because of a lie they'd told. Most importantly, the crime rate in those days was extremely low and air conditioners were rare, so it was common for people to sleep with their doors open during the summer. My mom and dad would often say, "That's it! We sleeping on the porch!" To their surprise, other neighbors would be on the porch laughing and sleeping in the summer breeze as well.

We were poor, but we had the best games. We played jump rope, double-dutch and played in the neighborhood playground. Our bright yellow home sat between the community graveyard and the playground. Everyone was like family, and it was cool.

Since I was the new kid in class with other fourth graders who appeared to have known each other for years, Ms. Makuz, my grade school teacher, asked me to introduce myself to the class. My classmates seemed to be members of families that were more stable than mine because there was little to no communication in my home. I was an abnormally shy child, which made it hard to make and establish friends in school. I was astonished that this was what my mom believed a *better life* was supposed to be.

Ms. Makuz would constantly embarrass me and the other four black students who attended the school comprised of 200 Caucasian students as if embarrassing us was better than telling us what she truly thought of us. When one of us did not know the answer to a math question, she would make us write the equation on the chalkboard and stare at it with our faces as close to the board as possible without actually touching it. One day, Ms. Makuz made me stand so close to the chalkboard that sweat filled my face. One of my male classmates asked Ms. Makuz if he could take my punishment for me, but she told him, "No, Sabrina will stand there until she gets it right." Over three hours later, after all of the other subjects had been taught and it was time for lunch, Ms. Makuz allowed me to abandon my stance in front of the board. The other students ran ahead of us to the cafeteria, so Ms. Makuz continued to verbally abuse me as if the daily torture of nearly sinking into the chalkboard wasn't enough.

"You dumb, stupid black! Does your mother ever help you with homework?" she screamed as she waltzed over to my desk and slammed my math book on my hand. Later that day, the other four blacks, Justine, Kendra, Parker, Palmer, and I made a pact that we would all sneak the answers to one another so we would never have to suffer chalkboard torture again.

CHAPTER 2
A SEED OF HATE

I was an overall friendly, open, honest, and opinionated child before we moved. Sometimes, I was too opinionated. My mother and father were very involved in church activities since we attended our family church. My father was a deacon, a bus driver, and a Sunday Night adult Bible class teacher. My mother sang in the choir, sang solos, and played the piano.

At the age of six, I was excited that I'd learned how to spell *no, yes,* and *go,* so I every time someone asked me a question, I spelled my response. However, because we lived in a dysfunctional household, I don't believe my parents were aware of how to embrace my personal growth. They never took interest in sitting down with my sister and I to find out what gifts, skills, and abilities we had. Children whose personal growth is not embraced during their childhood typically become either over achievers or attention seekers.

I had an aunt who called every-so-often to ask if my dad was home. On one occasion when my dad was not home, I decided to respond to my aunt's question by both spelling and pronouncing the word *no* to show her I'd learned how to spell. In her opinion, I was being a smart aleck, so she threatened to tell my father as opposed to praising my spelling. Instantly, my palms and body began to sweat.

My mother told me, "Learning to spell or not, Sabrina, you don't use spelling as a way of answering any questions."

My sister, who is two-and-a-half years older than I and was the only person I felt truly understood me at times, grabbed my hand and told me, "I understand, and I am very proud that you can spell." Her words were very hard to appreciate because I knew what the punishment would be once my father got home. When he got home later that evening, I receive a harsh beating for simply showing my family that I'd learned how to read.

As a child, I felt we lacked balance. We were either going to church, coming home from church, or coming home from church only to eat and go back to church. Church was the center of our lives. I probably would not have minded as much if the experience was nice; however, because my parents were an important link in and supporters of the ministry, things spilled into our household. My father, who was an attention seeker because of his childhood, often felt unimportant so being a deacon allowed him to feel important and accepted.

My father was an extremist when it came to ministry. Every Sunday like clockwork, my mother would wake us up at

6:00 a.m. to press our hair and get us dressed. By 7:00 a.m., my dad would scream at the top of his lungs to my mother, "Joyce, I told you to be ready by 7:00 a.m. or I am going to leave you!"

She would scream back, "Leroy, give me 15 minutes!"

He would respond, "No! I'm leaving," and drive away only to get up the street, turn around the corner, and come right back. We'd run out of the house every Sunday without having eaten breakfast, to rush to pick-up church members who would ask my father to wait patiently while their children grabbed breakfast.

One day, after attending a three-hour long church service, my sister and I only had a thirty-minute lunch break before we got on the twenty-passenger church bus to drive a long distance to another church service. For a six-year-old child who was born sickly, I was overwhelmed. After all, I had been up since 6:00 a.m. and had only had a thirty-minute break and one meal and was riding with twenty other people who were having multiple conversations very loudly. I developed the worst migraine a child could possibly have. Finally, I screamed at the top of my lungs, "Shut up!" My mom replied, "Sabrina, are you crazy?" Everyone sided with me and told my mom, "Well, Joyce, we were a bit loud." Well, I know once my mom got upset, and my dad sided with my mom, that meant I would have hell to pay once we got home.

Somehow, my name seemed to get called often by family members who thought I was mischievous and my father's only source of 'dealing with me' was whipping me with a belt. My father was from the south, so he wore an abnormally long and thick belt, one that can be compared to the reigns worn by a horse to keep it in line. The belt was so long that it would wrap around my entire body with each lashing.

My sister, who was my saving grace, would often come to my rescue and tell my father, "Please don't beat her! She didn't do it! She was innocent!" We were known to others as Joyce's pretty little girls with fair complexions and long, pretty hair held together by silk pastel yellow and baby blue bows, but at our core we were two little girls who were slowly dying as the abuse and derogatory behavior intensified. My father became a monster to us all.

My grandmother was as much involved in keeping the peace between my mother and father as she was keeping the peace in the family. When we moved, no one knew what was going on. Our house was so huge it took up almost the entire street. In fact, there was only one other small home that sat next to ours.

We seemed blessed since we'd moved from a small, urban row home to a very large home in the suburbs, but there was always little to no food, and clothes were scarce. My father would beat my mother so horribly that her face would be distorted, then he'd beat my sister for jumping in, trying to get my father off of my mother, and in return got beat for assisting.

The church members who were once envious of me and my sister now laughed as the stress of the abuse caused all of our *pretty hair* to completely fall out. In fact, my hair had gone from being down my back to measuring an inch or less.

None of us talked about the abuse. It was as if what was happening to us was a figment of our imaginations.

In fact, because of the abuse, my sister who once was my protector had become my greatest enemy and now joined in with anyone who was against a child who just stopped talking completely.

The abuse caused me to cease communication. I stopped talking in class and at lunch. I only felt liberated on Sundays when I visited my godmother's house for Sunday dinner and played with my childhood friend and cousin. It was the only sense of normalcy I knew. My godmother would share the basic necessities, like an abundance of food, soap and clothes, with me. I would ask to spend the night on weekends, but soon the abuse caused the weekend visits to fade away. There was a seed of anger growing inside of me that no one knew was there except the Angry I.

CHAPTER 3
LIBERTY IN SONG

I was 11 years old when my aunt reformed the church choir by allowing everyone to audition for pitch and strength. "Ok, Sabrina, it's your turn. This is what I want you to sing." Seeing her eyes get as big as quarters scared me. Fear had become my natural response to everything. Instead, out of all the other children, she continued to feed me lyrics to sing.

Afterwards, she took me aside and asked, "Does your mom even know you can sing?"

"I don't know," I shrugged. I've always been in love with music. After watching dance shows, I'd run in my room and listen to music for hours, but I'd never actually tried to sing.

Later that day, my aunt approached my mother, who was known for being a songstress, "Are you aware that Sabrina can sing?"

"Oh, can she?" my mother responded.

"No, Sabrina can really sing and I'm going to put her up to sing," my aunt informed my mother. My aunt looked me in my eyes and told me, "You did real good today. I'm going to allow you to sing." I sung with the children and adult choirs, with my sister at church events, and at district meetings with thousands of people. To others singing was merely an awesome sound to hear, but for my sister and I, it became an outlet to escape from our crazy life.

One Sunday, they announced that singers were needed for a special event. Because my sister and I were always singing, we felt we were prepared to sing for the event. Different district leaders began to ask if we would represent their churches by singing at regional events. My sister and I were excited because, for the first time, we felt important.

Because we were extremely young and shy, people were nonchalant when we stood before the audience to sing, but somehow when our mouths opened our shyness ended and our voices left the audience flabbergasted. To see people's reactions to our powerful voices was timeless and made my gift worth it. Every time there was an event, my father, amongst others, would request songs they loved hearing us sing, and we would sing the songs from the depths of our hearts.

However, I sometimes wondered if my father heard what others did. For instance, after we returned home from an event, he walked me to a corner and told me, "Yeah, a lot of people said y'all sing good. You sound alright. Sabrina, you're good as a background."

"No, I'm a great lead singer," I protested, but he was adamant that I would be best singing background. That day I lost the zeal for singing just as I'd lost it for spelling and speaking, yet I knew I could always find God in song when I needed to reach him.

Something about singing gave me a sense of liberty and I knew there had to be more to a thing called liberty, being alive. I was in pursuit of it, and I had to figure out how to find it. It felt like everywhere I turned I was entrapped by people who were not only dysfunctional but did not have my best interest at heart. I knew I would have to venture out. I was eager to return to school in the urban neighborhood where I once found happiness.

After one of my mother and father's final altercations, a family member told us we could not stay there temporarily, overnight, or even until we were out of harm's way. Shortly after the altercation, we received an eviction notice, which left me with mixed emotions. I was sad because I saw my mother struggle for something she wanted her entire life, but I was also happy because the eviction was an opportunity to escape the abuse and for my mother to face the fact that my father was not the right man for her. However, as my mother began to pack in anticipation of being thrown outdoors any day, my father began asking if he could come to live with us at my aunt's house. "Where am I going to go? I have nowhere to go," he repeated to my mother. "Please ask her." Later that day, I heard my sister telling my mother that this was the ultimate state of disfunction.

When you're in the process of being evicted, fear looms over you because you're uncertain when the sheriff is going to come to remove you from your home. However, my mother somehow sensed that the sheriff would arrive later that day, so she begged my dad more than fifty times to stay home to load our belongings on the back of his pick-up truck and store them in a safe place, but he shrugged my mother off and left.

I stayed home from school because I was ill. At no later than 10:00 a.m., we received a hard knock at the door and the sheriff barged in. "Miss, you have ten minutes to pick up all of your belongings and get out." "But all my things are still here. Wait! Please wait!" my mother pleaded.

"Miss," he continued, "where is your husband?"

"I don't have anyone to help me," she responded. I kept shrugging at my mother's shoulders under her wing the entire time.

"Come on mom, let's just go."

"No, I'm staying right here," my mother replied. The sheriff became so enraged that he began to sling my mother's beautiful piano, clothes and everything else out of the door and onto the lawn while my mother screamed in the street, and I cried as an innocent victim caught in a crossfire. Once all of my mother's belongings were on the front lawn, she walked from neighbor to neighbor in despair hoping someone would have a heart to help. By sunset, a family member whom my father called to help us had finally shown up while my mother, sister, and I sat on our front lawn with our bags, boxes, clothes, and mom's piano.

Later that night, my father showed up at my aunt's home where we were limp and exhausted, both mentally and physically. "Where were you?" my mom screamed. "Where were you!" His excuse, as someone who held a high managerial position, was that he could not leave his job. What I thought would be a blessing was actually a continuation of some of the worst years of my life.

My aunt laid out the law, and with all those laws all my father heard was the fact that he only needed to give her $200 and she was happy. My father made $800 a week as a foreman, so my mother often wondered how we were evicted from a home where the mortgage was $400 a month and why there was always so little food in the home. Living with my aunt was no different. My father often fell short of paying my aunt the $200 a month, which caused my aunt to wonder where all of my father's money was going.

He began to take advantage of the situation. My aunt felt that three months should have been sufficient time for my father to get on his feet, which may have been the reason she charged him so little money to live with her.

My mother, sister, and I slept in one bedroom where there were two single beds. My sister slept with my heavy-set mother in one bed, and I slept in the other. My father slept in a small room with a shelf full of 100 boxes over his head. If he would have moved the wrong way in the middle of his sleep, the boxes would have fallen and injured him. As for my aunt, who never approved of my father living with her, considering his behavior, told my mother not to move a single box and let them fall on my father's head as far as she was concerned.

Going from a suburban home which took up almost the entire street to an inner city, roach and mice infested, clutter and debris filled home did not seem to bother my dad.

My sister was much lighter than me and was always seen as the wiser daughter. I was a tomboy who would play outside for hours while my sister, "the studious one," would study the bible for hours. Whenever there was a Bible challenge no one, not even adults, could beat my sister.

As for me, I was a brown-skinned, frail young girl surrounded by family members who were color struck. During the summer, my older cousin would take my cousins, neighborhood friends and sister, but she would not take me. As many times as my aunt begged her to allow me to accompany them were the amount of times that she took pleasure in saying "No."

On one occasion, while playing with my smaller cousin, my cousin's twenty-one-year-old mother, who was pregnant with her fourth child, picked me up and threw me down hard on the concrete steps because the smell of the marker my cousin and I were playing with agitated her.

I sat on my aunt's step, day after day, not saying a word, while being bullied by my older cousin who lived with my aunt and her children next door. Each day, I cried for my mother, cried about the physical and mental abuse, and cried about the dysfunctional behavior the adults perpetuated. One day, I wiped my tears and angrily awaited the day my mother would return home from the hospital.

My mother returned home; however, she was passive in the way that she dealt with issues; whereas, my father took what others said at face value, beat us first then asked questions later, which did not make sense to do after we'd already gotten a beating . I told my mother everything that happened to me. She concluded that it was time for us to move, but my father told my aunt and mother he needed a little more time to save. However, less than two weeks later, he somehow had enough money to pull up with a new vehicle and tell us to pack a bag because we were visiting his relatives who lived down south. The south was the one place I loved traveling to because visiting my father's relatives was my first experience of normalcy. I was able to experience how families were supposed to live and treat one another.

When we returned from our trip, my aunt gave us a 30-day notice to vacate her home and I was relieved. I felt like I had been living in a shell, going through the motions, and merely existing during our year-long stay at my aunt's house. Our lives had not become any better or any worse; we were simply existing. I was excited for us to have our own space again.

CHAPTER 4
IT JUST CAN'T GET ANY WORSE

Exactly one year and 30 days later, we finally got a new house. It wasn't the house my parents wanted, but they believed we could fix it up and make it our own. We didn't care whether the house was small or really large. Our homes had always been really nice because my mother always put her finishing touches on them. I mean, how bad could it really be? We were just happy to have our own place and, perhaps, a fresh start.

"Watch the step, Sabrina," was all I heard as I walked up the crumbling brick step into the inside of an "old fixer-upper" as my dad called it. The house had dark green and mustard-colored wallpaper, no rugs, and old appliances. My mom and dad slept in the attic, which they'd turned into a third bedroom, while my sister and I slept downstairs in an extension of the home which held two additional bedrooms.

My father began to paint, purchase new rugs and appliances, but for three years, he was unwilling to buy a new heater until my sister and I were almost diagnosed with having pneumonia. My mother had been using one kerosene heater in an attempt to heat the entire home. In addition to the heater, we slept in coats, blankets, covers and anything else we could find to stay warm, but it was still no match for the bitter cold. So, when the doctors took a test of me and my sister's lungs, they were filled with black caulk; a thick, coal-like substance that continuously filled our lungs.

One day, a relative asked my mother why he had not previously been informed of our living conditions. It took him less than one hour to fix the heater. My mother shared a few other things with him, like our lack of food, and the family member dared my father to not provide food and other basic necessities for our family again. Household meals increased from my father only buying enough food to last three days a week to eating chicken in the morning, the afternoon and at night. This was because chicken was the cheapest thing he could find. I bet the cashier wondered how much chicken one man could buy for his family.

My father made my mother believe that he grew up eating five bags of chicken a week, two cans of sardines with grits on Saturdays, and one gallon of milk with a box of cereal, so our family should too.

My mom started substitute teaching for about three years of us being in the home and finally my sister and I were happy. Then, my mother fell down three flights of stairs and I thought she would no longer be able to work. Months later, she told us that the doctor approved her claim for disability, so she would receive a disability check. I didn't know what a disability check was, but I was glad that it meant someone would give Momma some money once a month. I'd just graduated from the 8th grade, summer had just begun, and I didn't want to endure any embarrassment for not having any new clothes as a high school freshman. So, if momma couldn't earn a paycheck by working, then she should definitely get it from the government.

Summer had just arrived and my sister, the one person who'd kept me sane throughout the years of chaos, informed me that she would be leaving for college as soon as the summer ended.

I really did not know how to receive the news she had just given me, and for the first time, I took all of the anger that I hadn't known how to deal with on the one person I loved most. Although it hurts me to admit it, I fought my sister almost every day after receiving the heartbreaking news; however, she equally fought back to release frustration that was caused by the abuse she equally received.

Even though my mother received a disability check, she never had any money as my father demanded that she give him $500 towards the bills out of her $600 monthly check. She would have, as she admitted, given him the entire $600, but my sister, who was now an adult, instructed my mother to keep $100 and give each of us $40 per month for our school lunch. My sister became clever and started teaching me the system she had down to a science since she would joke about me taking her place in the household because she'd graduated from high school. "Mommy gives us $40 a month for lunch as a secret without daddy knowing. Daddy gives us $2 a day for lunch. That's an extra $40. Save your money. We have a cousin who works outside the high school with a lunch truck. When he sees you, because he is a sweet, generous person, he will give you a free lunch. Save your money because you're going to need it," she instructed.

One day, however, I went to the municipal welfare with my mother in order to receive Medicaid. The social worker pitied us and allowed us to receive food stamps after hearing the details of my mother's story. But, as soon as the social worker looked at me, she told my mother, "No, I'm putting the food stamps in her name." I knew the social worker and food stamps were heaven sent. This was my mother and I's secret. For the first time, a girl who was malnourished would be able to eat a three-course meal.

I soon noticed something unusual was happening with my sister. I couldn't put my finger on what exactly was going on, but she constantly looked over her shoulder as if someone was always watching her. Although she was still a teenager, my sister was well-developed. Our house was made like a home with an apartment inside of it. My sister and I lived on the opposite side of the main section of the home where the living area, dining room and kitchen were located. My parents' bedroom, a spare bedroom and a bathroom were located up the stairs that were in the kitchen.

Our front door was furnished with a mailbox, and there was another door located on the side of the house, which led to the bedrooms where my sister and I rested. Because I was young at the time, I could not understand why my father would wait until my sister took a shower to come to the side of the home and stare at her for about five minutes while she was dressing. I did, however, understand that my father's behavior would make my sister cry.

When she felt that she could no longer handle my father's torment, she told me, "Sabrina, come here. I have something important I need to tell you." "What's wrong?" I asked. Although I did not understand our family dynamics, I realized that my sister had become more than my protector. While living in a home where it was clear that I lived with a parent who was incapable of making clear decisions for her daughters, in my mind, my sister had become a mother to me. She continued, "Look, I know I wasn't supposed to leave for college until September, but I spoke to the counselor and they offered me a summer job tutoring the students there. I'm not going to take it. Instead I will attend a summer college program before school starts in the fall." "No!" I screamed. "No, don't cry," my sister continued, "I will try to come home every weekend to make sure you're alright, and I will bring you home money. Also, I'm going to give you my I.D. You're a brown-skinned me. They won't know the difference. Work the job in my name. The check will come, and I will cash it for you." "Okay," I agreed. I didn't know what to expect. After all, the same thing I couldn't pinpoint that was happening to her was also happening to me.

While I didn't know what to do, I tried to stay clear of it. I spent the majority of the first few days of my summer riding my bike and sitting on the porch. A few days later, I turned in the direction of a loud voice saying, "What are you doing here?"

"Oh my gosh!" I responded to the childhood friend with whom I attended the suburban elementary school.

"I thought you moved away?" she inquired.

"I did," I told her, "and lived with my aunt for a short period of time but now we've moved back on the other side," as I pointed to the dilapidated home.

"Well, I'm here," she said, "and you don't have to worry about sitting here alone again." I smiled. I was just glad I had a place to go and a reason to be out of harm's way. Every day for the rest of the week, she came to get me early in the morning and we rode our bikes on the other side of town where all of my suburban friends lived. It was like the best of both worlds. I would go to school with my urban friends in the fall and winter and play with my suburban friends in the summer.

The following week, my childhood friend informed me that she would be moving because her mother and her mother's boyfriend were breaking up. I worried the entire day. She was the first ray of hope I'd seen in years. The next day, she came by with a female friend she'd met named Tyra. I instantly loved Tyra's personality. She was the exact opposite of every friend I'd ever known. She spoke her mind. She had all the designer clothes, more than she knew what to do with. Tyra knew how to do hair. She was cool, and the funny thing was, her parents were just as cool as she was. I'll never forget when Tyra told me, "Forget the fact she's moving, I'm going to pick you up every day."

Tyra use to blurt out, "What's wrong with your dad?"

"What's wrong with my dad? You can tell something's wrong with my dad?" I laughed so hard I almost peed myself. Though I never shared with her the depth of the things I'd gone through, it was therapy to share the part I did share.

"You think my dad isn't crazy," she said, "He beats my momma too."

For the first time, not only did someone understand me, but she often told me not to apologize for being myself. She told me, "You know what your problem is?" I was scared to ask "what." She always seemed to have some type of off-of-the-wall analogy for how life was supposed to be. But, the funny thing is, no matter how off-of-the-wall it seemed, it accurately depicted the things I went through. "You know what your problem is?" she repeated herself.

"Whhhhhat, Tyra?" I laughed.

"I ain't got morals."

"What, girl? Why are you so crazy?" I asked.

"For real, I ain't got no morals, but you do. There ain't nothing wrong with you and don't let anyone make you think there is."

She was the absolute best friend I could ever have.

She said, "Where are your clothes? Where are your jeans? Where is yo' mannnn?

To all three of them, in a small squeaky voice, I said, "I don't have one."

After cracking up, she said, "Well, I know it's school time. You getting ready to go to high school. So, this is what you're going to do. You're going to borrow my clothes and bring them back at the end of the week. I'll wash them, and I'll give you more." I had never seen anyone with so many clothes. Tyra had two bedrooms and a portion of her attic that were full of clothes. "As for your hair," she continued, "I will do it for you once a week, and as for a man, please take this corny guy, Quincy, off my hand."

I replied, "Yes," to the first two suggestions, but as for a boyfriend, "No, Tyra. I don't know him, and besides I've never had a boyfriend before."

"Come on! I want his friend, and he keeps getting in the way. Come on, I'm going to show you how to get to his house, say hi, and that's all. He's desperate he'll like you."

"Well, gee thanks, Tyra."

"Come on, you'll date Quincy and I'll date his best friend."

What was I supposed to do? She was my best friend. Although, I remained a virgin, dating Quincy kind of gave me a boost of confidence. Quincy and I experienced innocent, "puppy love." He was the first male who told me I was beautiful, words I never heard from my father. I wasn't fragile "lil Sabrina" anymore. I went to high school 15 pounds heavier. I now weighed 110 pounds and was thin with cute hips.

CHAPTER 5
A SENSE OF FREEDOM

My sister returned home a week before school started to check on me. "Sabrina," she said, "Wow!" I had changed my hairstyle, gained weight and had new clothes. "What's gotten into you?" This new sense of liberty I found was what I needed to finally exhale.

My mother informed my sister that I had a new friend that I'd play with every day. "She stays all day. I asked the girl's mom if it was okay for her to play all day over there," my mother told my sister. In that moment, I realized I'd gained, through divine intervention, a family outside of my family as well as mutual friends I'd gained through Tyra. Tyra's mother acted as a second mom to me.

Well, my first boyfriend dumped me. I was pressured to "put out" and, well, I'd survived under pressure many times before, so letting him go wasn't a problem. Besides, I was having too much fun. Between weight gain, new clothes, new hairstyles and a confident attitude, I was ready for high school.

At least that's what I thought. Walking in the halls with hundreds of kids was no joke. I guessed I would go back to being quiet until I met a girl named Becky who was in my home room class. "I notice you've been alone every day. Do you have any friends?" Becky asked.

I replied "No."

"Ok. I'm going to be your friend," she said. Becky was loud and bold. For the first time during my high school tenure, my silence was broken. She laughed at people in the hall and laughed about the people who were in our class. She would laugh all of the time. She taught me that, outside of getting good grades and getting an education, I shouldn't take life so seriously-- laugh through it.

Now, the thing about Becky was that her mom was so in love that she rarely acknowledged Becky's existence. For instance, Becky and I went to a step show on my sister's campus and stayed in my sister's dorm the entire weekend. "I asked my mom if she missed me when I came back that Sunday," Becky somberly recited the conversation she'd had with her mother. "She said, 'gone where?' I said, 'mom I've been gone since Friday.' She said, 'Really? Where'd you go?'" I reminded her that we have to laugh through the pain. I'd finally met someone whose family was just as dysfunctional as mine. I now understood what it meant to laugh through storms.

No matter how bad things got with my family, it was fine because I was learning how to deal with it. Besides, I only had three more years to live at home and I would be free. Like my sister, I would be in college.

Even though I was in the tenth grade, sometimes the thought of being free was harder to grasp. I'd go to school during the week, and every Friday afternoon we'd pick-up my sister from college. On Friday evenings, we were trapped in our room acting as if we had no knowledge of what was taking place in the living room across from our suite. My mother would tell us, "Don't go in the main area for nothing at all." That was her way of keeping us safe while my father watched adult movies all night into the morning. The stench in the living room from my father masturbating throughout the night was enough to make you puke. What was even more sickening is, even if you caught him, he was unashamed.

My father's appetite for pornography increased, and when it did, his behavior in the home became stranger, causing my mother's head to consistently turn.

One day, my sister and I were home from school. I felt it was safe to exit my room because I was unaware that my mother had gone to the store. I approached the entrance of the dining room and caught a glimpse of my father holding his private parts in the front room. He ran from the living room to the dining room before I could run from the dining area to lock myself in my bedroom. My father caught me, slammed my head into the closet, and rubbed his private parts against my body. My sister raced to protect me. "You shouldn't have been in the way," he attempted to blame me for his immoral behavior.

The event triggered other incidents I'd pushed to the back of my memory. For instance, on one occasion, when I was six years old, I stood beside my mother as she cooked in the kitchen while my father sat on the living room sofa and begged me to come sit on his lap. My mother protested, but my father insisted I obey his request. He told me to sit on his lap with my legs spread apart while he gave me a pony ride. He moved his legs rapidly. My mother shouted, "Get down Sabrina! Get down right now." I didn't fully understand what was happening, but I knew something didn't feel right. Every vision of a girl who loved her father, who came home and went on long walks with him, who got piggy back rides from him, and who would run to the door screaming, "Daddy, Daddy" when he returned home to hear him respond, "Plant one right here" as he pointed to his cheek, faded away and was instead replaced with anger.

Immediately after the incident occurred, one of my teachers became suspicious because I had become visibly nervous, unable to focus, and afraid. I didn't know what to do or where to turn because I wasn't the only victim of incest in my family, and in similar situations, the abuse was brushed under the rug or the victim was called a liar.

How many more times did my mother ignore what was happening to me? And how many more violations did I try to erase from my memory? For example, when I was in the eighth grade, I had a best friend with whom I'd been friends for two years. Naturally, I trusted her. One day, she asked me to come over to her house. She introduced me to her 21-year-old cousin, Melvin, who had just gotten out of jail. "You're going to be my girlfriend," he said. I didn't take him seriously. After all, what would I have in common with him? He was handsome, but he was also 21. I stayed for an hour, then I went home.

A day or two later, Drenna asked me to come over again. We hung together all of the time, but this visit felt strange. She asked me to go down to the basement to help her carry laundry upstairs. I made my way down the flight of stairs to meet Drenna, but, after hearing a few whispers between she and Melvin, he came downstairs instead. Drenna locked the door as I banged on it and yelled, "Let me out, Drenna, let me out!" Melvin pulled me down the basement stairs and molested me for hours. I was so angry with Drenna that I never spoke to her again. How could she betray me? Months later, I heard Melvin was back in jail where he belonged.

My tenth-grade teacher decided she could no longer keep secret what my father had done and continued to try to do to me. I was afraid of what would happen to me if my father found out I'd told. My teacher decided that she would report the molestation to the school nurse who, due to the situation, became a great friend to me and insisted on telling one of my family members who worked at my high school about the issue.

The family member told two of my aunts about what my father had been doing to me. One of my aunts denied the accusations and the other aunt, whom we used to live with, did not comment on the accusations, but she believed I was telling the truth. She told me, "I just cannot tell you what to do at this time," and promised my secret was safe with her.

I decided to be open with my mother about my father's behavior. I discussed the perverted act with her as well as a dream I'd been having.

"Mom, I know it has to be true. I see things in explicit detail. You have to leave him!" I demanded. "You have to leave now."

"I can't leave," she said calmly. "Where am I going to go?" Somehow, that always seemed to be her response to the abuse my father put us through.

My anger had reached its highest level. Just who do these people think they are? What gives them the right to screw up a person's life? I combed through each detail of my life, where I'd lived, who my parents and family members were, where I worshiped, how I was abused, and having no heat or food. I thought about the time my mother begged my father to take her Christmas shopping. She spent a total of $100 on my sister and I, which was only enough for one outfit each and a simple toy for me. My father was so upset. On our way back home, he drove full speed over a bridge while threatening to end all of our lives. My sister screamed incessantly while my mother and father fought for control over the steering wheel. My mother pulled the steering wheel away from my father and demanded that he stop the car. "So now are you going to leave, Mom?" we asked as my sister and I shook and sobbed uncontrollably. Yet, nothing was ever enough to make her leave. Eventually, my sister and I lost hope in my mother.

I stopped talking to my mother and father. I was pissed off for being pissed on. The next two years, I went through the motions. I blocked out all of my emotions just to get through the days. My father would still beat my mom and my sister, who seemed to be the only adult in the house, would stop the fights, but I would simply ignore what was happening and leave the room. On top of the abuse we faced in our home, the church people teased us, and I'd ignore them and walk away from them too. I anticipated the day I didn't have to deal with any of them anymore. Anger was no longer an emotion. It was who I had become. I had become the Angry I.

CHAPTER 6
OUT OF THE POT AND INTO THE FRYING PAN

Welcome to college, my sister. My freshman year of college was my sister's senior year. My sister met me at my first day of orientation. She laughed at me as I was in total shock. I got lucky because my roommate did not show-up to school, so I had the dorm room to myself. I was given a card with $1,500 on it to feed myself for a semester. "$1,500?" I said to my sister in disbelief. "Yes. We're on our own," She replied.

"Let me show you the cafeterias."

"You mean there is more than one? I asked.

"Yes," she laughed, "and guess what?"

"You mean there is more? I can't bear it."

"Any money you have left after you pay for the dorm room, books and food, you get back at the end of each semester."

"No way!" I screamed.

"Yesssss!" she screamed back. I was in heaven and happy.

One cafeteria resembled a food court in a mall, and the other was large with a variety of foods and a meet and greet. There were free movies on Thursdays, step shows, which were always exciting, and even more entertainment.

Before I could establish my own set of friends, people knew me as my sister's little sister and that's exactly what they called me. My living situation became better, but even with people all around, I felt so alone, and I didn't know why. What should have been the happiest time of my life, I still felt depressed. I had allowed my parents to make a decision of me attending a college that was close to home, which meant I was free from the chaos during the week. However, on the weekend, my father would pick my sister and I up from school to take us back to the same church and lifestyle, which caused chaos in our lives. So it felt as though we were never totally free.

I had a really hard time feeling connected. There weren't many blacks on campus. There were maybe 200 black students out of the thousands of students who attended our school and half of them were already in a sorority or fraternity. Other students were trying to find out how to be in one and they seemed to hang in packs.

I received a phone call from an old boyfriend whom I was in a relationship with during my senior year of high school. At this point, I really didn't want him in my life. He had been verbally abusive to me and could never prove himself as being faithful. He called to apologize for everything he put me through. With all of his friends, ex-girlfriends and "biscuits on the side" gone to different colleges, he too found himself alone and thought, with no one in the way, he was mature enough to reestablish a relationship with me. After several rebuttals, I finally agreed to allow him to visit. When I arrived, I realized I'd become numb to his very presence and what he represented.

Nevertheless, feeling pressured to do so, I sat on the bed next to him to listen to the epiphany he had about life and what he realized was important. However, in anticipation of a response from me, there was a long pause instead. He broke the silence, "I thought this was what you wanted. I am trying to be with you." I sat still. "I understand. You don't have to say anything," he continued. I'm glad he had come to that decision on his own. As he hugged me, it seemed as if the very life was being sucked out of my body. I was drained just having him there. "There was too much that happened between us," he said. I nodded "yes" as he left.

As I contemplated our encounter, I became angry. Was this an epiphany or was I his last resort because everyone had left him, and he didn't want to be alone? Was I supposed to say, "Yes, you're right. Let's forget all the times you told me the only reason why you were with me was because you thought there was absolutely no way your ex-girlfriend would take you back, and your anger of not waiting to see if she would take you back before entering a new relationship has caused you to cheat on me?"

Was I supposed to be so lonely that I would agree to be in a relationship with him again? Everything I was once attracted to was gone; the fake curls in his hair, muscular body turned to flab, the hip clothes that were now more than a year old, the scent of his cologne that was once enticing, now sickened me. I was angry at the fact that he would even ask to re-enter my life.

I was no stranger to loneliness. I grew up in a household with little to no parent interaction. I would come into the back bedroom that housed all of my mother's algebra, psychology and childhood education when it became too hot to play outside. My mother would not know where I was for four to five hours while I wrote in my mother's algebra book trying to solve the equations.

My mother would say, "Oh, I was wondering where you were. Were you up here all those hours?" I would say, "yes," and she'd say, "ok," and walk out of the room. Not once throughout my entire education do I recall either parent participating in homework assignments. In fact, during my tenure at an advanced school, where racism was an issue and blacks were few, I would beg my mother, who was a substitute teacher and house mom, to help me with the subjects I struggled in. I couldn't understand why she refused repeatedly.

One day, I cried so bad after being made a mockery of at the chalk board, "Mom, please! Mom!" I begged for her assistance. "No, you do it," she replied. "Mom, I don't know how. Please, my teacher said you have to show me." "No," she retorted, "you sit right there and do it."

Therefore, being alone was not an issue, when isolation was all I knew. I did realize, however, that I had become depressed because, for the first time in four years, I had become friendless. I'd lost communication with my best friend who decided to live at home and attend community college, and I failed to make new friends. While I knew I had an opportunity to change my life after leaving a dysfunctional and abusive environment, I didn't really know what "normal" was supposed to be. It seemed as if the male friendships I attracted were one in the same. They were unfaithful and verbally abusive.

The end of my freshman year came, and I returned home. My sister, her friend, and I were talking about the desire for a mate and mid-conversation I blurted out, "By the end of August, I am going to meet my husband." They looked at me with puzzled faces. "Watch. By the end of August, I am going to meet my mate," I repeated confidently.

CHAPTER 7
THE POWER
OF THE TONGUE

Although my best friend and I drifted apart as we entered our adult lives, I made a friend that summer who lived close by. I knew that she and I would only be temporary friends but, hey, she had a car. Every day, we'd be gone from noon to evening. Most times, we would just ride around because she enjoyed getting dressed and driving to familiar spots to look for guys to communicate with. This was new to me but, for the most part, I enjoyed getting out of the house. It was an interesting experience; we were both black riding around listening to Spanish music as her choice of men were Puerto Rican. I think, in her deepest thoughts, she believed was Spanish too. I mean she was really fascinated with Hispanic culture.

One day, while we were driving listening to music, I told her, "It's not that I'm against this. I'm far from racist, but do you even understand the lingo they are singing?"

She laughed, "No, but I do know a couple bad words."

Lord, have mercy on us both, I thought to myself.

We drove around listening to Spanish music and looking for guys every day until it was time for me to return to school. I didn't feel attractive at all. I didn't have the same feeling of true belonging with her as I had with Tyra. One day, when I began to struggle with my lack of true friendship and was in search of someone who understood me, I visited Tyra. "What's wrong?" she immediately asked at first glance. "And who you been hanging with?" was her second question since my old, gloomy look resurfaced. Tyra always seemed to know when something was wrong.

"I've been pretty much keeping to myself," I replied.

"Ok," she repeated, "and who have you been hanging with?"

"Marletta," I responded.

"Oh, Bianca?"

"Who?"

She laughed. Tyra and Marletta attended the same suburban school.

Tyra answered, "Yes, we called Marletta, Bianca, in school."

"What?" I repeated to myself. That's Tyra for you, the analyst of dysfunction.

"Yes," she continued, "Marletta would never hang with people of her own kind, you know? The make-up of her friends were white, and the men she dated were Puerto Rican."

"Yes," I said, "and every day we ride around listening to Spanish songs with her not knowing three-fourths of the words they are singing. In fact, Tyra, we stopped to talk to a guy she knew, and he even laughed and said why are y'all listening to Spanish music? I don't even know what they are singing and I'm Spanish!" Tyra and I laughed until we were in tears.

"No wonder you're looking like that. No, but I'm serious, I'm just surprised that the two of you are hanging together. She has always been pretty stuck up. Hair done; nails done. You know pretty much the fake type."

"Well, you know," I said, "it's company."

"Yes," Tyra went on, "and how is that making you feel?"

"Well, I really don't say anything to the guys. I just don't seem attractive."

"And why is that? You just need a new hairdo. Come on!"

Tyra, whose entire family was into hair, sat me down and began to work her magic on my head. When she was done, she turned me around and I looked in the mirror. I no longer saw myself as a young girl but as a beautiful woman, a woman any man would be attracted to. "Thank you so much! Thank you!" I said.

"You're welcome," she replied, "tell her she's not the only one who can catch a man!" Tyra said as she winked. My newfound confidence wasn't about catching a man. It was about feeling good about myself for the first time. I had become a beautiful woman and hadn't even noticed.

I walked home from being at Tyra's and the looks and compliments I received were priceless. I saw myself as someone who had options and no longer had to settle. However, I questioned if I knew what valid options were and how to choose the right mate. I grew up with people who screamed at me about religion and who ended every sermon with us going to hell. I didn't know that you were supposed to pray about finding the right mate or ask God to give you the spirit of discernment and mature you so you can make the right choices. I only knew what others told me about God and hadn't yet developed my own relationship with him.

I only knew two things. I wasn't too sure about the college I chose to attend, and I had to find a way out of my dysfunctional household. I finally arrived home from Tyra's house and, as always, I received a phone call from Marletta. As usual, she was eager to go for our daily drive. However, she wasn't prepared for the 360-degree-makeover I'd gotten with the stipend I'd received from college. With my hair and make-up done and new clothes, I showed up at her door. I was dressed in casual, black biker shorts, a matching blouse, and a costume gold necklace and earring set. I looked good and I knew it. I humbly knocked on Marletta's door.

"Is Marletta home?" I asked her mother.

"Oh my gosh, Sabrina, you look absolutely beautiful!"

"Thank you," I said. "Marletta!" she called.

"Come here," she yelled. "You're never going to believe this! Look!" she said.

Marletta came to the door with a dropped jaw, "Oh my gosh! Look at her red lips, long china bob, and a coca-cola-body that's to die for! I'm not going out with her," she said.

"Are you serious?" I asked.

"Why?" she responded, "Look at you!"

"Go ahead, Marletta, she wants to go out with you," her mother said repeatedly. After that day, she never asked me to go driving with her again.

It was the last day of August, and I decided that I was my own woman. While no man is an island, I had the ability to create my own destiny. I walked to the corner store, where I was stopped by a very nice-looking, Hispanic man, who was 10 years my senior. He sat in the driver seat of his BMW while he talked to his friend, who sat on the passenger side of the vehicle.

"Wow," he said, "She is beautiful."

I took a chance. "What is your name?" I was shy and new to this. After all, the two boyfriends I'd had were introduced to me and I was practically forced to be with them.

"Well, my name is Carlos, Carlos Rivera," he continued. "But because I am named after my father, everyone calls me Junior." Junior was tan with tight soft curls, green eyes, and bowed legs. I'd never dated outside of my race. He asked me, "How would you feel about dating a Puerto Rican?"

I replied, "Love has no color. I am not racist. I just believe in treating one another with love and respect." Hearing the words come out of my mouth was shocking. Love, honor, and respect was the theme of my sentiments, none of which I had ever witnessed or experienced.

"Well," he said, "I have tickets to a baseball game for tonight. I'm going with my friend here and his girlfriend, but I don't have a date. Would you like to go?"

"Yes," I replied, although I was no baseball fan. It was my first real date. That evening, Carlos chose to pick me up in a really old, beat-up car that smoked. I stood staring at the car with confusion. His BMW was so nice. *Ok, Sabrina,* I thought to myself, *You can end things prematurely, or you can move forward as planned.* I decided to move forward and did not realize how much one night would change my life forever.

"Well," he admitted, during the baseball game, "My friend says you may have been more into the car than you were into me, so I decided to drive my work car to pick you up. After all," he said, "You are a much younger woman." We laughed.

"Well, I am more into getting to know you," I replied. We both laughed at his little trick.

The reality was that he was a much older man. I was 19 and he was 29. Later that night, after leaving the baseball game and taking me with his friends to shoot pool, he admitted that, he himself, had just gotten out of an abusive relationship some months ago. He had recently bought his first home and wanted a loving, normal relationship, and he wanted that long-term relationship with me. I kept repeating, "Ten years is a long time to have been with someone. Are you sure you are ready for another relationship?" He assured me that he was ready to move forward.

Later that day, my sister and her friend wanted to know how my date went. To me, it was just a date, just talk. I believe I downplayed the date because of everything that had happened in my life. There was still so much rage inside of me due to me having unanswered questions. But to my sister, who was more spiritual, it was a ray of hope.

Her friend agreed, "Well, she said by August 31st she was going to meet her mate."

That day, I learned 'the power of the tongue' meant that we must be careful what we speak because it will come to pass, so be anxious for nothing. I agreed to be in a relationship with Carlos without really knowing much about him. No one had ever talked to me about how to choose a mate or what to look for in a mate. I didn't know anything about being equally yoked either. I learned that I was his complete opposite. He had a really good job but drank with his friends on the weekends. I remember telling him that he didn't have a relationship or know God, and I didn't know how to please him. He replied, "What's really wrong, Sabrina?" I mentioned to him that my life was in no way perfect, and it involved me being molested several times and living in a dysfunctional home. Carlos insisted that, despite my upbringing and parents' beliefs, I was an adult who was capable of making my own decisions. "I will be your protector now and I promise you, you never have to go back," he said. "In the meantime," he continued, "I will take you back to school for your sophomore year. I will come visit you once or twice during the week, and on the weekends, you can stay with me." It seemed like my only way out, so I agreed. Just as he promised, Carlos picked me up every weekend. "Where would you like to go out for the weekend?" he would ask.

"I don't know. Where can we go?" I replied in disbelief. This was a totally different lifestyle. I went from a life of little-to-no food to a man who took me to the finest restaurants, took me to the mall, and introduced me to designer clothes, shoes, and handbags. I didn't want for anything, and anywhere I wanted to go, we went. Eight months later, Carlos asked me to marry him, and I was delighted. The agreement between my father and I was that I would return home to live until I was married.

I spent all of my time with Carlos, and he promised me he would never allow anything to happen to me. Most of my time was spent in school, and on the weekends, Carlos and I went on elaborate dates. However, I'm not sure how much time I'd spent actually getting to know Carlos. For the first time, I was developing a prayer life. Although we set a wedding date that was three months from the date he proposed, I was developing a relationship with God and was now depending on God for answers. Be careful what you ask for. I asked God for answers, but I'm not so sure I was prepared for what he was going to show me.

A few days after accepting his engagement, Carlos picked me up, as usual, to go over to his friend's house to watch tv, shoot the breeze, and drink a beer or two. On this unforgettable Friday evening, his friend showed us a kitten he bought for his small children. The two-month-old kitten displayed behaviors indicative of it being in heat. His friend decided to take the kitten away, but before he had the chance to do so, Carlos took his leather glove and slapped the kitten repeatedly against its back to help the kitten masturbate. The more his friend and I yelled for him to stop, the more he laughed and continued to slap the kitten.

Traumatized by his indecent behavior, I started to walk home. Carlos drove to find me.

"Sabrina," he said, "I can't believe you would get mad at such a thing."

"Just the thought of your doing that, Carlos, reminds me of my father's behavior."

"I'm sorry, Sabrina," Carlos said. "It was just a joke. It will never happen again. I love you, Sabrina."

"Ok, Carlos," I replied.

However, that night, my words, "It reminded me of my father," kept replaying in my mind. But, we proceeded to plan the wedding. Was that a sign that I was supposed to call off the wedding? I was angry with Carlos for his actions and pissed at the enemy who made me feel like there was no way out, but living with Carlos, as opposed to my father, had to be a better option. He failed to inform me that he'd ended an eight-year relationship with a woman, whom he had assumed a father-figure role to her two small boys. In fact, he was the only father they knew, so telling his ex that he was married enraged her. She came to our home several times to burst windows, threaten to fight me, and kicked the doors. She called and left us harassing messages twenty-four hours a day. So much for my knight in shining armor.

Who and what I needed was evident. I needed the Lord.

CHAPTER 8
WHO'S YOUR DADDY

I reached that conclusion after the first week of being married. I knew I was going to need to be anchored in Christ, and I would need major support that would not come from my family's church. I resigned from the Pentecostal church I'd attended from birth and joined an apostolic church. I remember the first message I heard preached over twenty years ago. The pastor said, "You don't need anyone preaching to you about Hell. Can anyone tell me how to get to heaven? You can go to Heaven."

Oh, my gosh, I thought. I can actually go to heaven. Attending a church where you're related to everyone meant everyone either knew, or thought they knew, everything about you. Aunt Arby remembers the first time she hung your diapers, cousin Betsy knows you for all the lies you told, and Aunt Keira always monitored every boy who looked my sister and I's way. (I can't tell you how many lies were told on my sister and I who were virgins).

My life was already absolutely crazy, and by making the decision to marry Carlos, I had hit rock bottom. The man who confided in me that as a child he'd watched his father raping his mother, was now coming home from the bar at 2:00 a.m. and 3:00 a.m., physically abusing and raping me. One night, he came in so intoxicated that he threw up for hours. I held his head, wiped-up the mess, prayed for him, and put him in bed.

I concluded that I no longer needed God to just save me from my childhood, family tortures, a life of isolation or a bad marriage, I needed God to save me as an individual.

My new church was much different than what I was accustomed to. Pentecostal churches were very organized. Everything was time sensitive. Morning services started every Sunday at 11:30 a.m. and by 2 p.m. we were on our way home. The apostolic church I attended believed in letting the Holy Spirit have its way. There was no telling as to how long devotions would last. They were often two to three hours long. The preacher would then get up at 1:30 p.m. and preach until four o'clock or five o'clock in the evening. I didn't care. For the first time, I felt God. I was game for whatever was going to change my life as I knew it.

Soon, Carlos began to question the number of hours I was spending at church. After a month of my attending the church, I invited him to see for himself. I thought nothing of it as he attended my previous church with me; however, after an hour of service, he started pulling at his hair, shaking, and screamed at me, "I can't take this anymore," and demanded we leave.

My family knew something was wrong with me, but they didn't exactly know what I was going through. In fact, no one knew. Several months after getting married, my sister decided to move to New York to pursue a career as an actress. I pursued a more independent route; I got a job, my driver's license, and my first car since Carlos had decided he would no longer be responsible for getting me home from church.

My father bought me my first Cadillac. Shortly after, I talked to my father about how bad Carlos had been beating me. His advice to me was for me to try to "stick it out," but if it got too bad, I could come back home. Two months after driving my Cadillac, Carlos's ex-girlfriend stole my parked car and totaled it. After 18 months of marriage and during my junior year of college, I quit college and moved back home. My father cosigned for me to get a brand-new vehicle.

I was very worried about how my life would be living at home again. I hadn't lived at home full-time in three years. However, shortly after he received a shocking diagnosis. My father had cancer. I thought it was a little cruel for my sister to recite a prophecy she'd given my father about him developing cancer, but I had to softly admit to her that she was right. I only remember my father being hospitalized twice. The occasion my sister spoke of was when my father was hospitalized for two weeks. He'd given my mother permission to pick-up two of his weekly paychecks. I'd imagined that for a black man with minimum education during the 1970s, a full-time, weekly paycheck would have been about 200 dollars a week. My father advised my mother to leave both checks unopened, but because we were facing an eviction, my mother opened the checks and was shocked to find that the two checks totaled more than twelve hundred dollars. My mother took some of the money to buy food. After forty-eight hours of my father being home from the hospital, he beat my mother from the front room, into the kitchen, and down a flight of steps that led into the den area for opening his paychecks. He also beat my sister for screaming at him and trying to use a broom to get him off of my mother.

My mother, whose face was swollen and black and blue screamed, "Don't worry, he's going to need us one day."

My father screamed, "I will never need any of you."

At once, my sister, who was always very spiritual, looked back, pointed at my father, and told him, "God said you will die of cancer, and you will need us."

After three years of being in and out of the hospital, my father came to me and cried in my arms as he'd been given only three months to live. He asked if I could drive him to South Carolina to see his family one last time. He wanted to go badly, but my father was completely broke. He lived for his job, but he was demoted from a foreman to a regular employee and given a small pendent for 25 years of service to the company. I had just bought my first car, so my sister gave my father 100 dollars as spending money once he got to South Carolina, and I covered the gas and tolls. When he returned from South Carolina, the doctor told him the pollution-free air was what his lungs needed, which added three additional months to my father's life.

Shortly after returning from vacation with my father's relatives who had no idea how sick my father really was, he took me out on the front porch to share his financial despair and need for help with the bills. By this time, I was a manager on my job. However, when my mother informed me that one of my father's coworkers and long-time friends visited her to inform her that my father had several shares in the company, but my father, knowing he was going to die, chose to keep the paperwork in his work locker and refused to share it with his wife, the woman he'd spent 30 years with. Therefore, instead of assisting, I chose not to give him a dime and walked away. I would take care of my mother, but he needed to be left alone with his thoughts since, even in his last hours, he did not make the right financial and marital decision.

One month before my father's passing, I asked to speak to him. I was determined to not allow him to leave earth without discussing what he'd done to me. He sat and listened as I poured my heart out. He bowed his head in shame and did not comment. I walked away. Thirty minutes later, he knocked on my bedroom door. "I just wanted to leave you with something, Sabrina," he said as he handed me a broken VCR. In that moment, I realized that my father, who grew up with a mother who was too sick to raise him and not knowing who his father was, was just as broken as the gift he gave. I decided to forgive him, for my own well-being, and refused to allow him to die with the demons he refused to set free. I also realized that, although I wasn't properly fathered or protected as Carlos promised, I had a heavenly daddy who I could turn to no matter what.

In his last days, my father lost the ability to walk. He was hospitalized for three weeks. His last request was to die at home, where he eventually died in my arms. My mother was left with nothing except for the money from a life insurance policy she'd struggled to pay on her own. By the time we showed up at my father's job a few days after his death, his employer had cleared the paperwork; his coworkers admitted he'd hid. My mother was cheated out of hundreds or possibly thousands of dollars. After all, my father worked as a manager for well over twenty years and invested in the company from the time the company started and grew nationally.

Carlos promised he would come to the funeral. Besides, we were still legally married. Carlos showed up over an hour late. On the way back to my parent's home, he confessed that he was late to my father's funeral and ashamed of not being on time because he was with another woman. His admission of guilt set me free from the bondage I'd suffered at the hand of every man who'd hurt me.

CHAPTER 9
FACE TO FACE WITH MY DEMONS:
LET THE HEALING BEGIN

Demons of the past, everyone has them. I certainly had my own to deal with. For the first time in 25 years, my mother was free of my father's presence, and while she didn't have millions of dollars, she had enough money to live comfortably. My sister and I were adamant about not accepting money from her. We wanted to see our mother happy for the first time in our lives. Although, I would have been willing to take a back seat to her happy ending. As horrible as it may sound, there were many individuals who were relieved that my father was gone. I thought we could live freely by putting all of the bad memories behind us. Although grieving is normal, I had 25 years of grief and anger towards my abnormal life to sort through. My mother went into an extreme depression, which I thought would fade away over a period of time.

Instead, about a month after my father's death, I began to see a shift in my mother's behavior.

"Are you ok, mom?'" I said.

"Yes. Your father used to take me to a special doctor to get medicine," she said.

"What kind of medicine, Mom?"

"I don't want to go into details. I just need for you to drive me to the doctor. No big deal."

I was prepared to do anything to help my mother; however, when we got there, she insisted on me waiting outside. Her request seemed bizarre, but I did as she requested. Thirty minutes later, my mother came out of the door with a bottle full of medication. *Wow, that was fast service*, I thought. *This physician must be well aware of my mother's medical needs.*

I needed to further investigate my mother's behavior. Perhaps this would give insight into the lives we really led and bring both healing and closure to the anger I held inside. I went to visit my mother's oldest sister, the aunt whom we'd lived with. There was always the smell of something good cooking on her stove. It didn't matter what she cooked; she had the ability to make even the simplest dishes taste great. She would often take turkey or chicken scraps and make a thick, homemade gravy. Then, she would make homemade, buttered biscuits that would melt in your mouth and pour the turkey with gravy in the center.

"Aunt Mamie, there is something going on with my mother, and while I would like to think it is contributed to the death of my father, something just doesn't seem right."

"Tilley wit," as she often called me, "Sit down." Aunt Mamie had nicknames for all her nieces and nephews since she did not have any children. Therefore, we were all her children. I was the youngest. I inherited my nickname from her at a young age.

"Aunt Mamie, that's just it," I said, "I am no longer the same frail little girl. I need to know the truth."

"I understand baby," she said, "Sit down."

"Although people would like to think your mother's mental health issues were based solely on your father's abusive ways, that's untrue," she said. "You see, before your grandmother died, she had a talk with me. She asked me to take care of your mother. I told her I was sure she would be fine. But your grandmother told me, 'No, you don't understand.'" My aunt advised that my grandmother, who had my mother at an old age, explained to her that my mother was always mentally challenged as a child.

I was so disturbed; I called my sister on the phone. It's not that I doubted Aunt Mamie. If we ever wanted to know anything that was going on in the family or family history, we would just ask Aunt Mamie, but I didn't know if I was truly ready to deal with the secrets. "Yes, it's true," my sister said. What was true, and just what had my father hid from us all these years? If I was going to have to deal with a mother who was crazy, the least he could do was prepare me for it.

"It's not only true," my sister continued, "but the father you knew was angry." My father relocated from South Carolina to New Jersey. He was raised by an aunt and a man he knew as his uncle. However, my father's *uncle* called him a week before he died and divulged that he was, in fact, my father's father. After receiving this information, with no more than seven dollars in his pocket, my father hitched a ride up north from two of his cousins who decided to move. He slept on cold floors and often went to bed hungry because he had no one to love or support him.

One month after moving to New Jersey, my father found a job, and three months later, he was introduced to my mother by his cousin. My mother sold Avon products at the time. It was the only job my grandmother allowed her to have. She was the only one of her female cousins who was not married, and, due to my grandmother's strictness, no one ever thought my mother would ever marry. Even in her 20s, my mother was only allowed to sit on the front porch unless she was going to church or participating in a church-related event or activity. She never had a boyfriend and those who showed interest in her past the dating phase were turned away by my overprotective grandmother. I believed that, perhaps, my mother's lack of socialization contributed to her nervous behavior that, in-turn, increased to something deeper. Nonetheless, selling Avon was therapeutic for her. In fact, she would walk one town over to sell Avon and experience the added peace and solidarity. It was in that suburban town that she met my father's cousin.

However, my sister added light to my mother and father's story. "Mother said he was attracted to her because of our grandmother. He loved *nanna* because she was a God-fearing woman, church mother and preacher's wife. She was also a businesswoman, and each day there was always a spread of food on the table. Everyone knew her for her kind acts. He looked at her as the only mother he knew," she said.

There had to be some truth to the story as my sister told it. Before my father passed, he kept saying, "I loved your grandmother, but she tricked me, she tricked me." Things were beginning to make a little more sense. I was often told that one of the reasons my father didn't live with his natural mother was because she herself was mentally ill. My father thought meeting my grandmother was a blessing from the Lord. He always told us that, until he met my mother and began going to church, he didn't know about the Lord. He was a chain smoker and didn't have any sense of direction.

He would visit my mother every day. She fed him and prayed for him. Whatever conversation took place between my nanna and dad, he felt good about deciding to marry my mother. In actuality, he married the ghost of his past. My father married his mother, a woman who was incapable of taking care of her child. He resented his decision, so he figured he would abuse us instead, the seeds of his marriage and constant reminder of his decision. When we were young and my nanna was still alive, he would tell my mom that he would have left her if it wasn't for his children at least once a month. When my nanna died, my father abused us every time he thought about his decision to remain married to my mother. He hated her. He hated the fact that my grandmother never told him that the woman he was committing to was schizophrenic. Despite all of his faults, he promised to cover her by keeping her secret. Both family members and my mother's siblings were unaware of her disability until my father died. The only other people who knew about my mother's illness were my grandmother and eldest aunt.

With all the doctor's appointments I'd taken my mother to and with the medication, she shared with me that her deepest fear was that we would never forgive her. I questioned her reason for bringing up all the things she recalled had happened to us and why she had not recalled them before now. It is almost as if she could never acknowledge the lifestyle we were living as children caught in the crossfire of domestic violence; however, now that my father had died, her demons would not allow her to rest. She said she needed the medicine to cope. That day, I hugged my mother and forgave her. With a long sigh of relief, I was no longer angry with either of my parents.

CHAPTER 10
RELATIONSHIP CYCLES

Shortly after my divorce from Carlos, I began dating Michael. Michael was the complete opposite of Carlos. I went from being well taken care of to having someone who was very dependent upon me. For the first time, someone needed me, and for the first time, I'd become the rescuer. I was an educated woman who agreed to date someone, who admitted he'd only been out of jail for less than six weeks, was living in a one-bedroom apartment with his father, and had an income of only 75 dollars a month. The fact that he was kind and appeared to be incapable of hurting me was enough.

Two weeks after dating Michael, he asked me if I could loan him 75 dollars to add to the money he'd saved to buy himself Timberlines and he would pay me back in two weeks. I asked Michael how would he survive if he used his entire check on boots. The fact that it didn't matter should have raised a red flag. Actually, it should have screamed immature.

Truth is, perhaps we both were immature. We were both the youngest of our siblings and had never lived completely on our own. I was full of potential, however. Due to my life' circumstances and poor choices in men, I devoted time to pushing past those obstacles to gain a better life for myself while Michael made poor-choices in friends and went the other way. One thing was for sure, our common denominator was that we both came from abusive households. Unlike the two-parent household I'd come from, Michael's mother was a single parent of seven children, who worked two, sometimes three jobs. He recalls the eldest child being 16 years old when she began leaving the children home alone all day while she worked.

Michael admitted that he would have starved if it hadn't been for school lunches. One summer, his mother left them home alone for a full day with nothing in the refrigerator except for a can of diet coke that she dared one of them to touch. He'd often take a beating for drinking the soda. "It was just too hot," he said regarding the 100-degree day. "If I wasn't receiving a beating for that, it was for climbing out of the house window when she wasn't home to go play with my friend whose mother fed me lunch daily." Yes, Michael and I understood each other.

Michael had to see his parole officer every week. The parole officer's stipulation was that Michael get a job. I guess we both shared that stipulation. The one thing I vowed I would never do is take care of a man. After seeing him mope around his father's house for weeks, I told him he had one week to get a job.

"Don't leave me," I recall him saying.

"One week," I repeated.

"But what if I don't find a job?" he said.

"Then I'm gone," I answered.

I remember buying a Sunday newspaper for him, circling some jobs, and telling him to get up to fill-out applications and attend in-person interviews. On Wednesday, Michael called me excited that he'd gotten a job. "I was so scared you were going to leave me, Sabrina," he said. "I was thinking, 'please let this man hire me.'"

I was thinking, *let him hire him too.* He needed me.

Michael and I were a team, and we did everything we could to support one another. Every day after work, I would go over to his house and, when I wasn't at his house, he was at mine. A year later, Michael and I were engaged. *Things would be different*, I thought. It was an opportunity for two people who'd faced struggles in life to be different. Everything was normal when Michael and I were together. However, if I were to go to happy-hour with some of my female coworkers on a Friday evening, I would see a slight shift in Michael's personality. "I could have put on the music and made you a drink," he'd say.

I saw more evidence of Michael's mood swings prior to us marrying. He knew how long it should take me to get home from work, so if it seemed I'd done anything before getting home and preparing to go see him or calling him, he would often call me and ask why I had not called. Because he'd changed, I did not give as much thought to the incidents as I should have.

Finally, about a month before we married, Michael and I attended premarital counseling. The pastor, who eventually married us, prayed about Michael's jealousy during one of our counseling sessions. I never thought Michael was a jealous man, or maybe I just hadn't paid much attention to his behavior.

Determined not to feel as if I had failed again and that everyone was right in saying me and Michael would not last, I decided to tell everyone that I slipped on a broken piece of a sidewalk in front of our apartment complex instead.

A new job and a few months later, I found out, although physicians told me it would be impossible, that I was pregnant. I believed I would never have a baby due to endometriosis. Six weeks later during my first ultrasound, the ultrasound technician told me the baby did not have a heartbeat. My reaction to the situation was slow. Why would He allow the impossible to happen only to take it away?

I remember coming home and explaining to Michael that we'd lost the baby. This news devastated the both of us. That night, I cried while lying on the floor. At that moment, I heard God say, "Get up, brush yourself off." Whatever I'd done wrong to cause this miscarriage, I made a vow to God that I would correct my behavior. Days later, I went to visit a physician my mother suggested since I'd had problems conceiving a child too. I cried inconsolably during the physician's assessment. "Sabrina," he said, "having a baby is like rolling dice. Sometimes you get a bad one but shoot again. Next time, we will roll a good one." For the first time in weeks, I felt a sigh of relief. "Now, as for the reason for the cause of the miscarriage, Mrs. Brown, you're an anemic. That means there was not enough oxygen going to the baby's brain. I will treat you with iron pills for that. I want you to begin taking one capsule and vitamins to prepare your body for the future." Four months later, I received the most joyous news of my life. I was pregnant with my son Nick.

During my pregnancy, I tried to do everything right, even the things others viewed as being wrong. I was determined for this baby to survive. For nine months straight, I read my Bible two to three times a day. If I made the slightest mistake, I repented several times for it. I was going to present myself spotless and give God no other choice than to bless me. My husband was very loving while I was pregnant. Actually, my pregnancy was the only time he truly showed his love for me. After all, we both wanted a child. I stayed home and took care of the house while Michael worked full-time and went to school. I believed my life was perfect. During my eighth month of pregnancy, Michael came home and told me he had quit his job.

"What made you do that?" I asked.

"I'm never going to get ahead there," he said.

Hiding the anger I held inside, I asked Michael, "What are we going to do for money?"

"I don't know. I will think of something."

His *something* was leaving his full-time job to work a part-time job at a local supermarket. Three weeks later, he injured himself on the job and was unemployed again. Six weeks later, I gave birth to a healthy baby boy. God had to be pleased with me.

Not long after that, Michael received a job working at a shoe store rather quickly. It was not a fancy job, but the money he made was awesome. "Who makes 800 to 900 dollars a week selling shoes?" we often joked with him. Even his father thought it was awesome how Michael would assist three or four customers at a time. Michael loved the high-volume environment. He loved the hustle, which he said reminded him of his days on the streets. His supervisor acknowledged him for being the best salesperson on the team. I thought Michael's income would allow us to have enough money to buy a home and create a better life for our son. Like my father, five years later, Michael opened a separate bank account, and despite the one-thousand-dollar-a-week paychecks, there was very little food in our kitchen. Each week, I had a hard time figuring out what we were going to eat while he worked all day and ate out.

Six months after my son's birth, I dropped Michael off at work before attending church. Church was just what I needed. I needed God to change my situation. I was ten minutes late arriving home from church due to traffic.

"What are you doing being late?" he screamed.

"Didn't I tell you?

"What time did I tell you I got off? Don't you ever do it again," were his words. That night, Michael physically abused me in the car, and something inside of me died. Our relationship would never be the same again.

Two months later, I got a job. The pay wasn't much, but it afforded the basic necessities for my son and I. I continued to look for a job, and exactly one year later, I found an excellent one. I went to the interview in Michael's old beat-up station wagon. He insisted that I take his car instead of my brand-new vehicle. I listened to the music all the way to the interview while I prayed the car would make it.

"Hello, how are you?" the receptionist politely greeted me.

Wow, I wondered. *Could the people actually be this nice?*

"Let me give you a tour while you're waiting," she stated.

The building had marble floors and a staff lounge with free cappuccinos and drinks. Everyone seemed very friendly with one another and appeared to love where they worked. This was the environment that I longed to be a part of. They hired me on the spot. I finally believed God had a better life in store for me. Just as I thought, my coworkers loved where they worked, and I did too. They made me feel like I was accepted. The CEO thought I was a great employee. At the end of my second week on the job, he gave me a one-thousand-dollar bonus. I worked as many hours as my employer needed me to, and I didn't mind. I made friends in every department, and I felt as if I mattered. Life was great. I was eager to hit my monthly goals. My monthly commissions were one thousand dollars in addition to my pretty good salary. The more money

I made, the more I began to feel as if my days of being married to Michael were numbered. I was fed up.

Michael's job went sour as his employer now saw him as being non-compliant. Months later, Michael came home, and the baby and I were gone. I had put my needs first, and Michael's unemployment, depression, jealous behavior, and immature ways no longer mattered. I had no sympathy for the mistakes he continuously chose to make. He made excuses for everything, so I had grown tired of arguing and blamed his inconsistencies on a lack of common knowledge.

I moved into my own apartment. I was finally happy. I had enough money to buy my own furniture instead of someone providing it for me. Being able to experience the unconditional love of my son was priceless and being able to receive that love in a non-hostile environment gave me peace and serenity. Church, God, my adorable son, and my career was my focus. My baby made me want to become a better me.

Over the next few weeks, Michael was very apologetic. He missed his family. and against my better judgement, I agreed to let Michael move in. He promised to be a better provider and to make changes within our marriage, including having a joint bank account and doing things as a unit.

It was apparent that we'd never saw an example of a normal family, but I was willing to start from ground zero and learn.

We were one month into our honeymoon phase when Michael lost another job. Determined to be more of a supportive wife to Michael, I encouraged him to find out what his gifts and passions were and to trust that God had equipped him to live out those ambitions and dreams. I assured him that we would be okay, and I got a second job in the meantime to keep us afloat.

I realized that me being a better wife to Michael was not built on encouragement alone; rather, I needed to pray more, strengthen my relationship with God, who is my source, and make God the foundation of my life. One day Michael told me there was a job he was interested in.

"Ok, you're going to get it," I said.

"No, you don't understand, I applied for the same job three times," he said.

I turned to him, took his hand, prayed, and said, "I don't care how many times you applied in the past, this time you're going to get it." He was thankful, and together we believed he'd get the job. He and I had inherited a piece of land and had already taken the steps to build our dream home when Michael initially lost his job. "This was just a setback. It was not a denial. You will get the job, and when you do, we will move forward," I told him. He agreed, and for the first time, we were on one accord.

One week later, they called Michael and hired him. It took him six months, but he'd gotten the job he wanted.

Getting the job helped to increase Michael's faith. We now knew all things were possible. Michael had obtained the position through a temporary service and was willing to work hard to prove himself. Within a month, they hired Michael as a permanent employee. Michael developed a plan to obtain the mortgage we needed to finish the house we'd started to build. My credit was not that bad, and Michael had student loan debt, so he suggested we use the income tax refund and money from selling our furniture to pay off his debt so we could qualify for a mortgage. "Michael, this makes no sense. How will we live without furniture?" I asked. He insisted that after we used the money to pay off his student loans, we could immediately apply for our mortgage and buy furniture afterwards. I agreed. Two months later, I came home and all of Michael's belongings, my brand-new vehicle, and all of my money was gone. Michael used my money to purchase his own apartment. He'd stolen thousands of dollars from my bank account. I didn't have two cents.

Immediately after, I learned that I was pregnant with my second child. "God, what am I going to do?" I went to the leasing office to explain to the leasing associate what had happened.

"Do you intend to renew your lease?" she asked.

I instantly said, "No."

"Okay," she said, "We'll return your security deposit."

I left the leasing office, and for a second time asked God what I was going to do. God asked me where I would like to live, and my reply was that I really wanted a home, but I had no money. God told me to look for one. Later, I called a great friend of mine who owned his own business.

"You know, I am looking for someone to work part-time for me," he said. "You can work from home." I thanked him and decided that I would need to build my bank account quickly. My mom watched my son during the day while I worked. After work, I would pick up my son, Nick, make him dinner, and work my part-time job while he ate. I had one month to gain as much money as I could before my lease ended. I had found the most beautiful home, but I didn't have enough money to pay the security deposit. That night, my friend Patrick, who I was working part-time for, called. We had always been the best of friends. He asked how I was doing. I told him about the home.

"I will give you the money and cosign," he said.

"Can you repeat what you just said?" I asked in disbelief.

"I will give you the security deposit and pay the first six months of your rent. I just want you to be okay," he said. I knew Patrick's help was a gift from God. I moved at the beginning of the following month.

Michael and I had agreed that he would come pick up our son every weekend. One day, I received a mid-week phone call from him. I thought the call was strange because it wasn't Friday or Saturday. Michael told me he'd lost his job. His car was about to be repossessed. He was one month away from being evicted, and he had been starving for the last few days. I made it clear to Michael, who was still legally my husband, although I'd filed for divorce, that I would give him one bag of groceries, but he was no longer allowed to live with us. "It's over," I said. During the fall, I gave birth to the most beautiful baby girl, Mia, the apple of my eye.

CHAPTER 11
LIVING LIFE
WITH PURPOSE

The closer I was to being divorced, the angrier I became with God. I could not understand how God could use me to minister to and counsel other women who were like me while I was going through this situation. Dozens of women would walk up to me and tell me about their relationships. I met a woman who shared that her husband had been out of the country for a year. We believed, in faith, that her husband would return to the United States and their marriage would be restored. Both prayers came to pass, and the couple bought a beautiful new home together. I met a man who had been divorced for several years and through my prayers, his marriage was restored. I was angry that I had not received the same favor.

I was beginning to feel hopeless; my life was crumbling before my very eyes. I turned my face to the wall, and with my hands lifted, I surrendered my will to God.

At that moment, I heard God say, "I am going to use you."

I thought, *Okay, where's the punch line? I know you have always blessed me at the most inconvenient times just to prove to me who you are.*

"I am going to take everything that the enemy threw at you and use it for ministry. I am going to use everything that you went through to qualify you."

At that moment, I understood what it was like to be in relationship with God. I wanted to know more about him. He began to remind me about all of the gifts he'd given me. I'd forgotten how I used to sing in front of thousands of people. I had forgotten about the pastor who had ministered to our congregation and told me that I would be a counselor.

In the Book of Jeremiah, God said, "Before I shaped you in your mother's womb, I knew you, I predestined you." I searched for a greater understanding of this scripture through the word of God.

"So, what you're trying to tell me, God," I said, "is that none of the things that my father or mother did was included in your purpose and plan for my life?" I continued, "Before you even placed me in my mother's womb, you had a plan for my life? I was on your mind, and there is an expected end for my life?" I knew that my life depended on my relationship

with God. Jesus would be my support and guide. I didn't
know what life held for me, but I had to find out.

My past was so messy. Who would believe me? I didn't
come from a happy, two-parent home with a father who loved,
protected and mentored his daughter, loved his wife, and
encouraged his children. I wasn't born of a mother who knew
how to raise her child, protect her child, and lead her daughter
into womanhood.

God showed me that I would help saved the life of a single
mother who was abused, a teenaged-male who was sexually
abused by his father, and a young, teenaged-girl who tried to
commit suicide. God told me that there would be marriages
that he would use me to restore. These are but a few people
God caused me to encounter. I knew that God was going to
need to heal me in the process. The Lord told me, "There are
too many cracks. I am going to rebuild the walls in your life."
"You, Lord, are the potter and I am the clay. I rest in your
hands," I replied. Life did not begin to change immediately.
As a struggling single parent, I was homeless, had experienced
lonely nights, had problems finding childcare, and had
financial trouble. I knew God was my resource, but I
wondered why these things were happening if God said my life
would change. I was beginning to think God was failing me.

In 2010, at the age of eight, my daughter became ill as soon
as we returned home from vacation. She complained of cold-
like symptoms and vomiting. My mother had come to live
with me, and after two days of my daughter being sick, my
mother suggested I take my daughter to the hospital. I kept
asking her if she needed to go to the bathroom, but she was not

urinating or eating. I immediately picked my daughter up to slowly walk her from the bedroom towards the front door. By the time we reached the front room, she fainted in my arms. I raced her to the nearest hospital, and she was immediately taken to the back to see a doctor. Her face had become pale.

The doctor advised that he believed that my daughter may have caught a virus that was going around, but he would still recommend she get a MRI. I stepped away from the room to speak to one of my best friends, and the nurse approached me in the middle of our conversation.

"Ms. Brown," she said, "I have bad news. The MRI shows your daughter has a tumor which has erupted. A children's hospital that specializes in her type of illness has already been contacted. They are sending an ambulance for her and will ship her to their hospital to medically treat her."

"God no, no!" I screamed. My best friend immediately left her home to accompany me to the children's hospital.

Less than an hour later, we left the emergency room to transport my daughter to the children's hospital. Instantly my prayer life and level of faith shifted to another dimension. God instantly answered. He took me from asking him what I needed him to do, to seeing it come to pass. This situation was happening too fast for me to sit and be a student. The word of the Lord says, "They were healed as they went." I was going to have to shift to an active faith, which would cause me to speak the word of God over her life. I began to speak as the scriptures declared, "She shall live and not die to declare the work of the Lord," I would say. However, within several hours of being at the hospital, she was "code blue."

She was immediately rushed into surgery. There was a small church in the hospital. I took the cloth the Jews use for healing, placed it around me, and went to the altar to pray. While I was praying, I saw an open Bible. God led me to the scriptures that depicted the life of a priest and how the priest and his household would flourish. I had learned that the tongue can speak both blessings and curses, and I had the power to speak things into existence. Since God gave me that word specifically for my child, I was going to speak that word into the atmosphere. One hour later, I went upstairs. I was greeted by the doctor with great news. They expected the surgery to be much more complicated, but the tumor was benign and removing the tumor was not a complex process. A shunt was placed in her head to drain the fluid from her brain and she was admitted into the Intensive Care Unit (ICU). Within her first hour in ICU, she had an allergic reaction to the seizure medication she was given. I had never experienced anything like this situation. The doctors could not get her to respond. I asked if I could lean up against her and hold her. She would not respond to the doctors or to her name being called, but I leaned against her ear and whispered the name, "Jesus." Immediately she opened her eyes. The doctors advised that they had never experienced anything like this. A week later, my daughter was released from the hospital.

Prior to leaving the hospital, the nurse stood up and gave me instructions. "I want you to know that you have a miracle baby," she said.

"I know, thank God for a praying family."

"You don't understand. Did the doctors ever talk to you about the type of tumor she had? I want you to look at the diagnosis. This is a rare tumor. You are born with it. You don't know you have it because it shows no signs of being there until it erupts. Ninety-seven percent of children who have it do not live. When you took her to the hospital, the tumor had already erupted. The doctors did not want to alarm you, so they decided not to talk it over with you. They could not understand how she even lived through being transported from one hospital to another," she informed me.

She is definitely a miracle.

I told myself that I could get through anything in life if I could survive my daughter nearly dying. The shunt was removed from my daughter's head and the doctor advised that she no longer needed the medicine she'd been taking. God told me my daughter would never have to go through anything similar to what she'd faced again because of the priesthood and calling on her life. She needed to be around to perform the work he'd called her to perform. Later that week, with her head wrapped up and stiches still in place, she asked to ride her bike. I notified the doctor, and he thought it was amazing that she felt up to it. He told me to watch her carefully, put her helmet on and allow her to perform her normal activities.

God taught me, through my daughter's illness, the difference between asking for a blessing and speaking a blessing. There will be challenges in life, but when you know who your source is, you believe that God will cause everything to work together for your good.

CHAPTER 12
AUTHENTICALLY SABRINA NE'CHELLE

G od's glory causes you to forget all that you had to go through to get where you are. I continued to work in career development and human resources motivating students and employees to establishing a better life for themselves. I also counseled women on relationship issues, including abuse. God took me through several challenges, healed me from them, and still allows others to benefit from what I survived. I guess that's the way life is sometimes. We can't choose the life we're born into, but we can learn from it and make better choices.

I didn't understand why it was important for me to spend time alone with God. No relationship, just he and I. I learned that the majority of my issues were due to the fact that I didn't really know who I was. I mean, I thought I did. I knew who my parents were, what my up-bringing was like, and I knew plenty of my maternal and paternal family members. I knew that I could tell you about all of the mistakes I'd made in life. I could tell you about all of the dreams I had, yet I could not tell you who I was or who I was destined to be.

God had to show me exactly who I was designed to be and the reason why my life was so hard. He showed me why the enemy sent so many distractions in my life. Part of the enemy's plan is for us to never come into the true knowledge of who we are. Jesus said to his disciples, "Who do you say that I am?" It is important that you know who you are. Part of the reason why we choose the wrong mate is because we choose our mate based on where we currently are in life as opposed to where we're going. Then, when the right man or woman comes along, if we know enough about ourselves, both physically and spiritually, we will recognize our God-sent soulmate. Jesus walked with twelve disciples, yet only Peter answered, "Thou art the Christ, the Son of the living God" to Jesus' question. Christ gives Peter his inheritance based on Peter's revelation. Jesus told Peter, "Upon this rock will I build my church and the gates of hell shall not prevail."

What was Jesus saying to Peter? Knowing who you are releases your inheritance. When you receive a revelation about your life's purpose and identity, the enemy cannot stop you. He can throw darts in your way, but he cannot stop you. It is for this reason that David said, "I fought the lion and I fought the bear." Sometimes, you have to send a message to the enemy to let him know you fought the lion and the bear. You have gone through every obstacle and you won. God shared with me that my dreams and ambitions were actually visions he had given me involving the gifts he'd blessed me with. These gifts are indicative of my true essence and are meant to be shared to bring God glory.

Moreover, Jesus also told Peter, "The gates of hell shall not prevail." The enemy can never stop what you have been assigned to do. He can try to slow you down by throwing distractions in your way, but he cannot prevail. The Bible says, "He who has begun a good work in you shall perform it." Everything happened with a word. With his word, God formed the entire universe. He spoke the same word and formed man. The word that was planted in me from birth, was a seed. The enemy tried to choke the word by making me think I would never survive living in an abusive household, going through crazy relationships, and having a dysfunctional upbringing. I was born to sing, write, and host a relationship talk show.

The word of God says, "The whole earth moaneth and groaneth for the true sons to appear." God had to teach me that my past did not dictate my future. My parents and my past did not matter. Not even my last name mattered.

I am Sabrina Ne'Chelle, and this is the story of my life. I am no longer the Angry I. I am entering the phase of my life where I no longer focus on the past. I am healed from situations and people that the enemy added to my life. God used those same people, places and things to make me stronger, to give me victory, and to allow me to be able to counsel women from being a victim to being victorious. I've learned that forgiveness is not for others; it's for ourselves. Whether someone asks for your forgiveness or decides not to, be free. Remember, your next level, the abundant life you want to live, and your healing depends on it. It's not where you start, it's where you finish. I am no longer the Angry I. This is just my diary, the only evidence of what used to be.